Marion Schmid

MUNICH

It all began with the monks . . .

The first document referring to the town goes back to the year 1158. At the Augsburg Imperial Diet in that year — on the 14th June, to be precise — the Emperor Frederick Barbarossa sanctioned a crime that by any standards may be regarded as a violation of international law. Duke Henry the Lion had the Bishop of Freising's bridge across the Isar near Föhring burnt down and the ancient salt road diverted over a new bridge.

Why this "Munichen", as it was called, or "zu den Mönchen" ('place of the monks'), was not destroyed again in 1180, as the Imperial Diet had decreed, nobody can say.

Henry had fallen into disfavour in the meantime, and no one was prepared to speak up for Munich at the Regensburg Imperial Diet. Nevertheless, the decision to raze the place was not carried out, probably because the Bishop of Freising had begun to show his personal interest in it. For decades he carried on a feud with the new Dukes of Bavaria, the Wittelsbachs, to gain ascendancy over the town.

Munich only hesitatingly took over the role of royal seat of the Wittelsbachs — Ludwig II, called the Severe, occasionally held court here from 1255. On the other hand, the town grew rapidly in importance as a trading place. In about 1300 its population must have numbered roughly 3,000, while a few decades later there were already 10,000 people here. At the same time there emerged a class of self-confident burghers, who knew how to assert themselves in the face of the dukes and later the electoral princes.

Towards the end of the 13th century, the citizens of Munich were no longer prepared to accept the constant debasement of the coinage and made short work of tearing down the royal mint. There were also frequent clashes between the guilds and the merchant families represented on the city council.

The Old City Hall was built in 1472, almost at the same time as the Liebfrauendom ('Cathedral of Our Lady'). By this time the city already had over 10,000 inhabitants as well as independent guilds.

This was a high point in Munich's history and coincided with the first attempts by the rulers to expand their powers. In 1561, Duke Albrecht V extended the rights of his "princely city of Munich" once more, but at the same time pointed out to the council with an unmistakable threatening gesture that they were to moderate their demands or he would have to issue a decree considerably restricting their privileges and freedoms. Thus Munich's fate became more and more dependant on the wills of the princes.

A remark made by the Swedish king Gustavus Adolphus when entering the city as victor demonstrates just how impressive Munich appeared even after the ravages of the Thirty Years' War. Munich was a "golden saddle on a scrawny mare", he observed, and regretted that the residential palace of the elector Maximilian I could not be transported to Stockholm on rollers. However, his admiration for Munich did not keep Gustavus Adolphus from squeezing considerable financial "contributions" out of her citizens.

By 1794 the population had already passed the 34,000 mark and in 1806 the city became a "royal seat and capital" as a result of the liaison between the Wittelsbachs and the French emperor Napoleon. The obelisk at Karolinenplatz ('St. Caroline's Square') is an eloquent reminder of the price paid for that royal crown: in 1813, 30,000 Bavarians fell while fighting with the "Grande Armée" in Russia.

The city became the seat of the archbishopric of Munich and Freising in 1821. No less important as a milestone on Munich's road to becoming a real capital was the removal of the state university from Landshut to Munich in 1826. This period saw the population rise from 76,000 to reach almost 90,000 in the year 1834. As a result of local government reform outlying districts were incorporated into the city (Schwabing in 1890, for example) so that by the turn of the century the population reached 499,932, of whom admittedly only 180,000 had been born in Munich. The attraction of this "Metropolis on the Isar" cannot be more effectively demonstrated than by these figures.

After the easy-going atmosphere that is said to have marked the era of the Prince Regent, there followed the First World War, from which over 12,000 men of Munich did not return. In 1918, the city became a particular focal point of international politics when Kurt Eisner called the Soviet Republic into being. Later in the same year Eisner was assassinated. The extent to which political terror both from the left and the right became a feature of Munich life is shown especially by the so-called Hitler Putsch outside the Feldherren-

Monacum

Münchhen.   Schedel: Weltchronik. 1493.   20 × 52 cm

Munich as illustrated in Schedel's World Chronicle (1493), one of the earliest pictures of the city

halle ('Hall of the Generals') in 1923. Even though this attempt at a Nazi coup d'état failed, it did not prevent Munich from being hailed as the "capital of the movement" in the National Socialist era that dawned in 1933. This ended in the nights of the blitz in the Second World War, when over one third of the city was destroyed.

Yet the optimism that has always been part of the Munich character — even if the people here do occasionally reveal a rather dour sort of charm — also won through after 1945. In 1958, at the time of the celebrations connected with Munich's eighth centenary, the popu-

lation numbered exactly 1,011,878. Munich had thus joined the select club of those cities with over one million inhabitants. Fears were expressed that the city might lose its unmistakable flair on account of this rapid growth, but they proved to be unfounded as, for example, the 1972 Olympic Games were to show, when Munich acted as host to people from all corners of the world. In the seventies and eighties, Munich became increasingly important as a suitable location for industry — not the kind of industry associated with smoking chimneys, but the kind that can provide the latest technology. In other words, Munich is looking to the future.

5

Bavaria's Capital on the Edge of the Alps

In most cases it is the foehn that is responsible for the wonderful view people living in Munich get of the Alps, which begin a little over 60 miles to the south of the city. This mild southerly wind may have real advantages, but people also use it as an excuse for being in a bad mood and for anything that does not go right.

Grumbling undertones are almost a trademark of genuine citizens of this city. However, they soon brighten up when they realize what a truly blessed piece of earth they have been granted to live on. Of course, like all metropolises the Bavarian state capital is only viable on account of the close links it has with its surroundings. What Brno once was to Vienna, or Silesia to Berlin, in the case of Munich that is Lower Bavaria in particular. One should not play down the fact that many new ideas also came from Upper Bavaria and the Upper Palatinate — Altbayern, the 'old heartland of Bavaria', as those regions are generally called, which does not imply any disdain for the people of Swabian or Franconian stock.

As a rule, however, the inhabitant of Munich looks to the south and the Alps. He does this not just because he likes to shin up a few peaks, or scoot down the slopes on skis, but because that chain of mountains just outside the city bounds is just as much a part of Munich as the Hofbräuhaus, beer or the glockenspiel. Upper Bavaria is in fact more than simply Munich's geographical surroundings: it is the soil in which the city is well and truly rooted.

The inner city with the "Frauenkirche" (Church of Our Lady), "Alter Peter", the Old City Hall and the Church of the Holy Ghost

St. Mary's Column in front of City Hall, with the towers of the Frauenkirche in the background

Well-known Landmarks of Munich

Mention has already been made of the monks. They gave the city its name and are still to be found in the Bavarian capital's coat of arms although the monk in a habit and carrying the Bible that Erasmus Grasser carved for the Old City Hall in 1477 has turned into a girl "Münchner Kindl".

Let us begin with the unusual tower that the citizens of Munich almost lovingly call "Old Peter". What makes this landmark unique is its architectural form: the rectangular lower part is capped by a vaulted structure, which in turn is crowned by an elegantly-formed spire. St. Peter's has only looked like this since the city fire of 1327, after which the two towers were joined to each other. At first, however, the pointed roofs were retained, and were only rebuilt to look as they do now in 1607. In spite of its baroque decoration, for which among others Johann Baptist Zimmermann and Ignaz Günther were responsible, the interior still clearly exudes the Gothic spirit.

Up to the present day the Frauenkirche ('Church of Our Lady') has remained the undisputed landmark on Munich's skyline. It had become necessary to build this enormous cathedral, constructed between 1468 and 1488 by Jörg von Halspach of Landshut, because "Old Peter", Munich's most ancient parish church, dating from 1181, could no longer accomodate the growing congregations, at least not without "putting the salvation of souls at risk", as

The Old City Hall at Marienplatz ('St. Mary's Square')
with a view of the Church of the Holy Ghost

an old document states. While enormous numbers of citizens were present when the foundation stone was laid by Duke Sigismund, ten years later their readiness to make financial sacrifices was exhausted and the completion could no longer be guaranteed. The churchmen of the city turned to Pope Sixtus IV for help, and he had a solution to the problem. Whoever visited the new cathedral between the first vespers on Laetare Sunday and the second vespers on Judica Sunday in the year 1480 was to receive complete absolution. 123,700 pilgrims brought in a total of 15,000 guilders so that Master Jörg was able to finish the construction. Even so, the money was insufficient for him to complete the towers, and Schedel's chronicle of the world, which came out in 1493, still shows the flat makeshift roofs. It was another thirty years before the "French bonnets" were popped on to the Gothic structure. Thus was created what has remained the real symbol of Munich until today.

Munich's population grew relentlessly during the 19th century and

"Der Alte Peter" ('Old Peter'),
the tower of the city's first parish church

The Gothic Cathedral of Our Blessed Lady,
the Munich landmark known throughout the world

The glockenspiel on the facade of the New City Hall

Detail on the porch of the City Hall

In the autumn sun in front of the City Hall

the figures rose from 40,450 in 1801 to 130,222 in 1861. Thus more and varied tasks arose for the local authorities resulting in a rapid increase in the numbers of people employed. This also meant that a new city hall became an urgent necessity. After 26 different plans had been put forward and discussed heatedly, the local authorities finally voted by a thin majority for the blueprint of the architect Georg Hauberrisser, and thus, as was stated, "for the Gothic style but with the proviso that manifold alterations are to be made to the plans." The foundation stone was laid by King Ludwig II on 25th August, 1867, and in the summer of 1874 the building was ready to be moved into. At first the people of Munich were not at all satisfied with their new city hall, and only the Association of Christian Artists found kind words for it. The critics of the city hall soon received support for their arguments since it turned out that the building did not meet the demands of a large and growing city. Thus extensions were begun as early as 1889. The 279-foot tower proved to be a particular point of contention, and its completion was delayed not only by strikes but also by those critics who believed that it might clash with the impression made by the towers of the Cathedral and the general harmony of Ludwigstrasse. Yet the councillors continued to support Georg Hauberrisser. In the new year of 1909 the rooms in the New City Hall were ready for use. The total costs were put at 15,507,794 marks, and that included the outlay for the site. The City Hall suffered severe damage during the Second World War so that after the currency reform a further 3.2 million marks had to be found before the building could be supplied with a new roof. It was also not long before the "Münchner Kindl" was looking down from the tower of the City Hall once again.

The New City Hall, built in neo-Gothic style

The Residence –
Seat of the Ruling
Wittelsbachs

"They knew that a village within the borders was more important than a kingdom miles away!" What Benno Hubenstein has to say about the "iron-fisted territorial politics" of the Wittelsbachs may also be applied to the attitude of these rulers towards their family seat. Once a territory had been acquired, the Wittelsbachs regarded it as their property, for which they were fully prepared to take up arms, even against their own relations. As a result, their lands came to be split up. This may have been detrimental to the outlying country and the people, but Munich itself has a lot to thank them for. Ludwig II, called the Severe, gained possession of Upper Bavaria, the Palatinate and Munich in 1225, upon which he made the latter his royal capital, while Heinrich continued to rule the Lower Bavarian lands from Landshut.

When one considers the manner in which Ludwig set up court in Munich, it becomes clear that he simply did not trust his surroundings. Even today one cannot fail to notice the fortress-like qualities of the Alter Hof ('Old Court'). It is a stronghold in Gothic style, protected by walls and towers, whose painted decoration of unusual diamond-shaped patterns only came to light again when war damage was being repaired. Its small oriel tower came to be called the Affenturm ('Ape Tower') because in 1282 a tame ape is supposed to have taken the duke's son out of his cradle and carried him to the top. Today, the magnificent mediaeval and Gothic buildings, of which the city gates (Isartor, Sendlingertor and Karlstor) and the Salvatorkirche ('St. Saviour's Church') deserve special mention, still dominate the map of the inner city.

The Grottenhof ('Grotto Courtyard'), a secluded little pleasure garden of the Residence, dating from the years 1581 – 1583

The New City Hall

The Old Court in the first ducal Residence (built in 1255)

However, it was not until the baroque and rococo periods that Munich's characteristic architectural contures really emerged. Evidence of this is to be found in buildings whose history nevertheless goes back to much earlier periods. To take one example, the Residence grew to reach its full extent over a period of about 300 years, from the mid-16th to the mid-19th century.

Without a doubt, the King's Building at Max Joseph Square is the most impressive part of the Residence. This wing, which was modelled on Florentine Renaissance palaces, was built between 1826 and 1835 in the reign of King Ludwig I. Here the baroque ancestral portrait gallery, in which there are 121 pictures set in elaborate carved gilt frames, is well worth seeing. It contains portraits of the Wittelsbach family from the dukes (1180 – 1623), followed by the electors of the period 1623 to 1806, through to the kings up to 1918.

The Residence had been considerably extended under the elector Maximilian I, who gave his stamp to the west face along the narrow Residenzstrasse. From here, one also has access to the courtyards of the Residence, such as the Fountain Courtyard with its beautiful Wittelsbach Fountain. The Cuvilliés Theatre, which is considered to be the finest rococo theatre in the world, is certainly a masterpiece of its kind. It was built between 1750 and 1755, whereas the wing with the Great Hall was not completed until 1840.

One of the many courtyards in the Residence, the Brunnenhof ('Fountain Courtyard')

The Grotto of Shells and Perseus Fountain in the Grottenhof

But let us return to the rulers with whom the history of the Residence is so closely associated, and go back to Count Otto, who was raised to the status of duke in 1180. He and his family were not thought to have much of a chance of reaching a position of permanent power. After all, the Wittelsbachs, who went under the name of the Counts of Scheyern up to 1115 and then took their name from a castle in the west of their extensive lands, were by no means the richest or greatest of the nobles. Yet many a critical observer was to be mistaken. From the very beginning this noble house managed to stay in power in spite of all the conflicts, both within its own ranks and with others.

In particular the female members of the ruling family played an essential role in this respect. Even before "Blithe Austria, go out and marry!" became a well-known saying, the Wittelsbachs had become past masters in political marriages. This began with Otto I, who was only able to enjoy his newly-acquired title for three years. His wife and particularly the Archbishop of Mainz, an uncle of the Wittelsbachs', made sure the heritage was not lost and acquired more and more allies by means of favourable marriages. Nor did Duke Ludwig I lack the talent of statesmanship when it came to choosing a partner. He not only led the widow of his greatest rival, the Count of Bogen, to the altar, but also acquired his lands and thus the right to use the blue and white heraldic diamond pattern. This characteristic was not restricted to just one Wittelsbach, as Otto, son of Ludwig the Kelheimer, showed when he acquired the Rhineland Palatinate by marriage and refused to relinquish it. This time the booty was the symbol of the lion in the coat of arms.

Tenacity, above all, is a basic quality of the Wittelsbach family. In Benno Hubensteiner's opinion, they were "quick-tempered and pious, incredible hunters, and brave into the bargain, of a temperament that was easily moved – like all Bavarians, in fact!" The grandson of the first duke, for example, owes his byname "the Severe" to his being involved in a sinister murder. His sons, Rudolf and Ludwig, took their rivalry to such extremes that from 1329 the Wittelsbach line was split into Rudolf's (the Palatinate and Upper Palatinate) and Ludwig's branches. However, the victorious Ludwig was able to leave a united Bavaria behind him when he died. His heirs became the overlords of Bavaria as well as Lords of Brandenburg, Holland and Tyrol.

However, it cannot be said that these successes were handed to Ludwig (b. 1287 in Munich) on a plate. As Alois Johannes Lippl stresses in his "Bavarian Eulenspiegel", Ludwig had acquired a difficult heritage when he was elected German Emperor after the victory over his Austrian cousin, Friedrich, at the Battle of Gammelsdorf in 1313. He became involved in the traditional conflict between the Emperor and the Pope, both with their claims to sovereign

King Ludwig II (1845 – 1886)

power. Yet, just as he defeated the Habsburgs a second time (in 1322), he also repeatedly insisted on his rights by opposing the Curia. He took things to such extremes that he refused to recognize the Pope, then set up an antipope during a journey to Rome and even crowned himself Emperor. This was all while he himself had been deposed as king by the Pope. The title "der Bayer" ('the Bavarian') was "granted" him by the Pope, not as a mark of appreciation, but rather of deprecation, even hate. However, the Wittelsbacher himself took the title as one of distinction.

Ludwig was clearly the first ruler to realize the importance of the newly-flourishing cities and their needs. For example, he had a wall built round Munich that was so forward-looking in its conception that it was able to stand up to the ravages of half a millenium. Ludwig also proved to be a progressive monarch in re-codifying the law. He was actively devout, and his conflict with the Pope was not an obstacle to founding the monastery at Ettal "in praise of Our Lord and in honour of Our Lady".

Elector Max Emanuel (1662 – 1726),
the State Collection of Paintings
in Schleissheim Palace

Two centuries passed in which the line was preoccupied with its own problems before it was again endowed with an outstandig personality, the elector Maximilian I. In the 15th and 16th centuries there were three parallel lines of dukes in Altbayern. Of the repeated conflicts with the citizens, one is of special note. In 1455, Duke Ernst had his daughter-in-law, Agnes Bernauer, drowned in the Danube near Straubing — simply for reasons of state.

Soon, however, the Ingolstadt line died out, and the Landshut branch appeared to be threatened with the same fate. Not wanting to submit without a fight, the Landshut line could not avoid entering upon a War of Succession (1503 – 1505). Munich won, and the wise duke Albrecht IV took over, intent on eliminating such hereditary struggles in the future. He achieved his goal. With the one small exception of the Neuburg Palatinate Bavaria was united for all time.

After this period of power politics, the Wittelsbachs began to reveal their artistic inclinations, even gifts. They devoted themselves to collecting art and books as well as extending the Residence in Munich. In addition, at Court they engaged Orlando di Lasso, a musician from across the Alps, and generally became patrons of the arts. During this period the state was running ever deeper into debt.

The royal crown on velvet, in the treasure chamber of the Residence — gold and gold-plated silver — Paris, 1806: M. Guillaume Biennais

It was therefore of benefit to the Wittelsbachs, Munich and Bavaria that one of the most important regents produced by the ruling family then came to power. The elector Maximilian I ruled for 54 years. Not only did he introduce a new system of criminal justice but he also freed the land from its heavy load of debt. He even succeeded in making impressive extensions to the Residence. And all of this in the midst of the Thirty Years' War. Maximilian was at the head of the Catholic League with Count Tilly from the Netherlands at his side. The house of Wittelsbach was doubly involved in this conflict. The Protestant "Winter King", a member of the Palatine branch, was in opposition to the Bavarian duke, a Catholic. Maximilian emerged as the victor and received the Upper Palatinate, which had originally been annexed by the Counts Palatine. On top of that he was awarded the title of elector.

The years of hardship were followed by an epoch in which the elector Ferdinand Maria managed to lure Italian master builders to Bavaria, where baroque influences were absorbed with such enthusiasm that they may now be counted as part of the of the typically Bavarian style of architecture. An especially fine example is to be seen in the Church of the Theatines, which Ferdinand Maria had built in gratitude for the birth of his son.

State coach, in the Marstall-Museum
('Museum in the Royal Stables')

That son was none other than Max Emanuel, who gave the Bavarians considerably less cause for joy than his father had done. The new elector "was extremely well endowed, both mentally and physically, clear and precise in his orders, if rather more of a dazzler than a deep thinker," as Lippl puts it. He sacrificed nearly everything to his ambition. As a young man he began well, helping to free Vienna from the Turkish siege. But then, risking some tricky manoeuvres between the great powers, he succeeded in losing his lands. After a period of exile in France, he returned to continue the construction of Schleissheim Palace. He was given the honorary title of "The Blue Elector" . He had a number of buildings put up in baroque style, and this was an allusion to their appearance.

In 1742, his son, Karl Albrecht, gained the imperial crown, but it brought him just as little luck as it brought the line of Ludwig, i. e. the Wittelsbachs, in general. After the death of the childless elector Max III Joseph, the heir came from Mannheim (1777). Karl Theodor of the palatine branch was, quite naturally, not enamoured of Munich. The feeling seemed to be mutual. Nevertheless, he had the English Garden laid out, opened the art collections to the public and had the Danube marshes drained. On the other hand, his successor, Max Joseph from the palatine line of Birkenfeld-Gelnhausen, enjoyed a great deal more sympathy. This honest, rather conventional man steered his country through the storms of the Napoleonic era, and in 1806 was made king by Napoleon. King Max I Joseph is mainly remembered for giving Bavaria a constitution, to which his son and successor, Ludwig I, also made an important contribution. During Ludwig's reign (1825 – 48), Bavaria and Munich experienced countless innovations, dramatic developments even: in Franconia (integrated into Bavaria after Napoleon) the first train ran in 1835, the Ludwig Danube-Main Canal was built, as well as the Ludwigstrasse in Munich, the Walhalla ('Valhalla', nr. Regensburg) and the spa facilities at Brückenau. Ludwig moved the University from Landshut to Munich and endowed monasteries that had been secularized by his father.

The Antiquarium of the Residence –
the official receptions of the
City of Munich are held here

When the king was forced to abdicate on account of a harmless affair with the dancer Lola Montez, Max II became King of Bavaria for 16 years, during which not only the sciences were promoted, but also folk music, wood carving and poetry.

Upon the death of his father, the 18-year-old Lúdwig II came to the throne completely unprepared for the task. He was to be the most popular and best-known of the Bavarian kings. Even when it was suggested that he should be declared unfit to rule before he led the land to rack and ruin, the people's affection for their Ludwig remained

unbroken. His three "royal castles", Linderhof, Neuschwanstein and Herrenchiemsee, are now great tourist attractions. Before the latter two were completed, Ludwig died in mysterious circumstances in Lake Starnberg on 15th June, 1886.

The following years under Luitpold, the Prince Regent, saw painting and literature flourish; he died on 12th December, 1912. The First World War broke out two years later and was to terminate the era of Bavarias's dukes and kings. On 9th December, 1918, King Ludwig III fled from his Residence, and Bavaria became a Free State.

overleaf: St. Kajetan's Theatine Church in Odeon Square,
built 1663–1675; the Hofgarten in the foreground

Present-day Bavaria still feels attached to its earlier tradition. The Bavarian Government has forged a link with the epoch of the kings by holding its official state receptions in the Antiquarium of the Residence. This 226-foot-long vaulted room was created by Wilhelm Egckl in the years 1569 – 71. It is considered to have been the first museum in Germany as it was intended as an exhibition hall for the ancient sculptures that in particular Duke Albrecht V had acquired.

"Café am Odeonsplatz" in front of the magnificent "Theatinerkirche"

"Hofgarten" of the Residence with Pavillion

A Place People Love and Where Life is Worth Living

Life can be really pleasant in this city. That is how one might sum up the extravagant praises sung in the fifties and sixties when Munich's slogan was "The International Metropolis With a Warm Heart", but probably the succinct expression "a village with a million inhabitants" most appropriately reflects the impression Munich makes on people. The combination of the large modern city with many native, even peasant, elements may certainly be taken as being typical of Munich. In the meantime the locals are as good at strolling and sauntering about with no particular place to go as many Latins, who are not slow to express their amazement at this feature of Munich life. Of course, there have always been fashion-conscious women here who are prepared to take upon themselves the exertions of window-shopping before recovering from their "efforts" in the famous cafés around the central shopping area.

Since the innovation of pedestrian precincts, many a Munich male has also found himself making a little detour in order to take a breather on a bench or to listen to one of the numerous street musicians, and even perhaps throw a coin or two into the violin-case.

Looking from Karlsplatz ('St. Charles' Square')
towards the pedestrian precinct formed
by Kaufingerstrasse and Neuhauserstrasse

23

Even at Karlsplatz ('St. Charles' Square'), which is also called Stachus and once had the dubious fame of being Europe's busiest traffic intersection, fountains invite people to linger a while without actually turning the place into an idyll. In fact this is where Germany's first pedestrian precinct was created, leading away from here towards Marienplatz ('St. Mary's Square'). When the inner cities were threatening to suffocate in traffic in the sixties, the planners came up with a new idea. With the construction of the underground railway, many shops at Stachus disappeared under the surface, resulting in advantages for both the traffic above ground and business below. Over the years Munich has attracted more and more foreign visitors, and the pedestrian precinct has played an essential part in this. It was here that the citizens of Munich were confronted with alien cultures and given a chance to show their oft-praised tolerance which they have done with considerable success, after a short warming-up period.

One citizen of Munich enjoyed great success all over the world so that his home-town put up a fountain in his memory. That was Richard Strauss. Its sculptor, Hans Wimmer, draws upon Strauss's greatest success, "Salome", and lets the Roman-style relief tell the plot of the musical drama. The nearly twenty-foot-high pillar is topped by a bowl, from which the water overflows so rhythmically that one feels one is watching Salome perform her dance of the seven veils. The constantly bubbling fountain forms an attractive contrast to the pronounced static character of the facade to the Jesuit College in front of which it has been placed. Incidentally, this facade is what remains of the whole complex built by Friedrich Sustri in the years 1585 to 1597. Not only the fountain but also St Michael's Church stand out effectively against the regular rows of windows.

Underground railway station beneath Stachus

The Karlstor ('St. Charles' Gate')
by night, looking towards Karlsplatz

24

*Street artists are an attraction
of the pedestrian precinct,
as are the numerous street musicians*

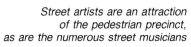

Shopping below ground at Stachus

Karlsplatz, also known as Stachus, with the Palace of Justice (built 1891–1897) on the right

The Richard Strauss Fountain,
created by Hans Wimmer in 1962

Refreshment and recuperation near the fountain

Food and drink
in the pedestrian zone

Shopping in Neuhauserstrasse

The Ida Schumacher Fountain, created by Marlene Neubauer-Woerner in 1977

The Liesl Karlstadt Fountain, created by Hans Osel in 1961

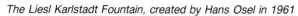

The Karl Valentin Fountain, created by Andreas Rauch in 1953

"We've got everything!" That is how Ferdinand Weissheitinger enthused about Munich over 50 years ago. Today he is still keeping watch to make sure things stay that way — as a figure over a fountain at the Viktualienmarkt ('Traditional Food Market'). Unlike his fellow-comedian Karl Valentin, who stands amongst the market women a few yards away inside an upturned question mark, Weiss Ferdl, as he was known, was capable of going into raptures, praising things to high heaven and expressing jubilation, but you never really knew when his words, to all intents and purposes spoken from the heart, might suddenly turn into biting satire. Nevertheless, Weiss Ferdl's rhetorical question as to whether there is a city anywhere on earth that unites as Munich does all the components that go towards making life so pleasant can only be answered with a clear "No". All great cities have their drawbacks, and Munich is no exception. Even so, it has remained a place worth living in, is even endearing, and we owe that in part to Weiss Ferdl and the colleagues in his profession, even after their deaths. The reference is, of course, to the fountains named after famous folk-singers. In Munich there are over 1,100 fountains — whether in state, municipal or private possession — either spurting water out of artistic forms or just prosaically gushing. It is worth making a trip to this city if only to search out all the different types of fountain that have managed to survive as witnesses to Munich's rich history or have been created by contemporary artists.

The Weiss Ferdl Fountain, created by Josef Erber in 1953

*Different types of
traditional cafes
in Munich and stalls
with tasty delicacies*

Liesl Karlstadt (Karl Valentin's partner on the stage), the folk-singer Roider Jackl and the gossip Ida Schumacher all clearly feel at home amongst the bustle of the Viktualienmarkt. So does Weiss Ferdl, of course. It is not by chance that the most famous characters of Munich's cabaret have been eternalized here. On the one hand it was around this square that the public houses were to be found in which Valentin and his like performed. On the other, the folk actors — in Munich certainly an honourable term — were in their element here in the midst of ordinary people, especially the market women. Ernst Hürlimann, Munich's leading caricaturist, along with Ernst Maria Lang, once told a rather significant joke on the topic of the Hofbräuhaus. At the beginning of the tourist season two labourers set out in order to exchange signposts indicating, for example, "To Munich 10 km" for ones saying "To the Hofbräuhaus 10 km". When

asked what they are up to, they reply rather artlessly, "To put an end to all the questions!" But, quite seriously, statisticians really claim to have found out that no other question is asked more frequently by strangers to Munich than how to get to the Hofbräuhaus.

And it really is rather hidden away between Tal ('The Vale') and Maximilianstrasse. In fact it is best to take one's bearings from the Old City Hall. From there Sparkassenstrasse ('Savings Bank Street') leads to a square that is so tiny that it is simply called Platzl ('Little

Munich's Viktualienmarkt, rich in tradition, where shoppers are attracted by fruit and vegetables from many countries

Invitation to traditional Munich restaurants

Square'). Incidentally, Platzl is also the name of a world-famous public house at which you can get Bavarian comic sketches, yodellers from Upper Bavaria and general high spirits all served up with your leg of pork and beer. This is where Karl Valentin and Weiss Ferdl, both already mentioned above, once took to the stage as comic actors, humorists or enigmatic philosophers.

The Augustines' beer garden

Hospitable variety and cosiness

The Platzl — that is to say the square — is dominanted by the Hofbräuhaus, of which not only the beer hall has achieved fame. Originally, people in from the country went into the lower part of the house. Nowadays visitors to Munich can hardly pass by without dropping in for a beer. The upper floors also house various bars, and in particular the enormous hall in which brass band concerts, not to mention dances in the Fasching season, are held. Further traditions connected with the Hofbräuhaus are the Schrammelmusik (music played by a quartet traditionally made up of two violins, a guitar and an accordeon) in the garden, and the fact that one may consume one's own rolls and sandwiches in the garden and the beer hall.

A snack in a Munich beer garden: there is nothing quite like it

The "Schwemm" in "Hofbräuhaus"

The world-famous Hofbräuhaus

The citizen of Munich has retained his love of the small things in life on top of his three great passions, Fasching, strong beer and the Wies'n ('the [Fair in the] Meads'). To take one example, he is crazy about his four-footed friends. The Zamperl-Brunnen ('Doggy Fountain') may be taken as proof of his love for animals and that he indeed feels close to Nature in all respects. Further evidence of this may also be found in the German Museum of Hunting and Fishing, which has been in existence since 1966 and is very popular with visitors. On display in the museum, which is housed in the former Augustinerkirche ('Church of the Augustines'), are Count Arco's well-known trophy collection as well as numerous treasures of art and culture, such as 500 native animals, a famous collection of weapons, glasses from Bohemia, or the collection of so-called Wolpertings (mythical Bavarian animals). The Museum of Fishing shows the development of fishing and equipment from the earliest times up to the present.

Along with a number of places of worship in Munich, the church itself was turned into a profane building during the secularization of 1802. It served various purposes before it came to form the worthy setting for the German Museum of Hunting and Fishing. Now the museum is known not only to Munich animal-lovers, but has made a name far beyond Bavaria's borders, especially when information is required about any aspect of hunting or fishing. The reason for the museum's reputation is to be found in the range of objects on display and in the special exhibitions which are constantly changing so that the museum can often make a contribution to discussions on the latest topics of interest. The collections themselves attract both the expert and families on a day out. In addition, the museum catalogue on the subject of hunting is a real must for booklovers.

The Zamperl-Brunnen, a fountain put up especially for dogs, shows that the people of Munich have a soft spot for animals

A large and friendly wild boar cast in bronze is on guard outside the German Museum of Hunting and Fishing

The Asam Church: this rococo gem was built by the Asam brothers in the years 1733–1746

A Walk Taking in Some of the Art and Architecture of Munich

Many of the inhabitants consider it to be the most beautiful example of its kind in Munich, even if — or perhaps because — one might easily overlook it: tucked away between the residential buildings along Sendlingerstrasse, the little church dedicated to St. John Nepomuk is certainly judged to be a jewel of Bavarian rococo. No less an architect than Egid Quirin Asam, also famous as a sculptor and ornamental plasterer, created something quite special here. In 1733, he and his equally well-known brother, the painter Cosmas Damian Asam, constructed their own church next door to their town residence.

Without a doubt the Ruffini House is also well worth a visit. Its facade both testifies to the great skill of craftsmen and also acts as a reminder of the Ruffini Tower, torn down in 1808.

A sign testifying to the long history of Munich craftsmanship

The architect Gabriel von Seidl was responsible for the construction of the Ruffini House (1903 – 1905) situated at Rindermarkt ('Cattle Market')

Apart from the Karlstor ('St. Charles' Gate') and the Sendlingertor ('Sendling Gate'), of the old Munich fortifications only the Isartor ('Isar Gate') remains, and that is in such fine condition that it could hardly be matched elsewhere. Thanks are due to King Ludwig I for the excellent state of the gate, through which one can reach Haidhausen after crossing 'The Vale'. In 1833 he commissioned Friedrich von Gärtner to renovate the ruined gate. While they were working on it the restorers discovered the fresco by Bernhard Nehr, which certainly enhances this construction with its twin towers. The fresco shows the "Triumphal Procession of Ludwig the Bavarian after his Victorious Battle against the Habsburg Frederick the Fair at Mühldorf in 1322".

A few pages back there was mention of the triumphs of another Bavarian, and, just as at the Viktualienmarkt, here inside the Isartor his memory has also been honoured. While at the former place a statue over a fountain acts as a reminder of him, here in the 'Valentin Museum' he comes alive and is tangible. The unique spelling in German of Valentin-Musäum with an "ä" shows that one should not approach this museum with the same eyes as one would countless other museums in Munich. Here is to be found the spirit of the most representative of all the Munich comedians, a master of confused

logic and a quixotic character. His frequent and desperate tilting at all kinds of windmills has been demonstrated in this "Musäum" at Isartor in a manner almost as brilliant. Thus Hannes König, the founder of this museum, gathered together everything that went to make up Karl Valentin's indispensible props and set it all out in a style closely reflecting the comedian's enigmatic sense of humour.

His top hat and his zither as well as the uniform Valentin wore when acting his sketch "Robber Barons at the Gates of Munich" were, of course, essentials. Nor did König forget the nail symbolizing the way in which Valentin said goodbye to a bourgeois existence, hanging his everyday clothing up on a hook, so to speak.

The fresco painted on the east face of the Isar Gate shows Ludwig the Bavarian entering the city

A painting inside the Isar Gate

The Isar Gate, part of the former wall round the city

The "Valentin-Musäum" in the Isar Gate

Dieses Gebäude
der alte Hof genannt
wurde erbaut
im Jahre 1253
von Ludwig dem Strengen
und war auch die Residenz
Kaiser Ludwig IV.

*Reminders of Munich's
rulers, master builders
and craftsmen*

*The Sendling Gate,
a part that has
survived of the
second city wall*

However, as already mentioned, the charm of this city also consists in its fountains. At Lenbachplatz ('Lenbach Square') the mighty Wittelsbach fountain roars as layer upon layer of water cascades down. In another place the 'Naked Daphne' presents herself full of natural grace. This city has indeed got something to suit everyone's taste!

Josef Henselmann's Cattle Fountain (1954)

The Old Botanical Garden with Josef Wackerle's Neptune Fountain (1937)

The lions by the steps leading up to the Feldherrenhalle are not simply looking down the royal boulevard, Ludwigstrasse, where it begins at Odeonsplatz. On the left, one has got his eye on the facade along Residenzstrasse. From this angle it becomes clear that when the Residence was extended between 1611 and 1616 use was made of painted architecture together with a facade divided into sections. The slanting gables of the portals

Karl Knoll's Fish Fountain (1884) at Marienplatz

Adolf von Hildebrand's Wittelsbach Fountain (1895) with statues showing the healing and destructive power of water

A modern fountain in the pedestrian precinct

The memorial to Count von Rumford, founder of the English Garden

The lion at the entrance to the Residence
opposite the Hall of the Generals

The Max II Monument

St. Luke's Church at St. Marianne's Square by the Isar

with the four cardinal virtues and the reliefs with their coats of arms stand out all the more because of this. The Feldherrnhalle itself was constructed between 1841 and 1844, being modelled on the Florentine Loggia dei Lanzi. Under the cover of its arcades memorials may be found to Count Tilly, the Bavarian commander-in-chief during the Thirty Years' War, as well as to Prince Wrede, famous as a commander in wars at the side of and against Napoleon. The Feldherrnhalle became more generally known as the result of a tragi-comic demonstration by National Socialist groups led by Adolf Hitler in 1923.

The citizens of Munich put up a monument to Count von Rumford, whose idea it originally was to lay out the English Garden and who managed to persuade the elector Karl Theodor to put the plan into practice.

St. Luke's stands out among Munich's Protestant churches. It is set in a smart residential area not far from the island in the Isar on which

the German Museum was established. St. Luke's Church also dates from the time when Oskar von Miller pushed through his plan to build a museum of technology and it was constructed in pre-Reformation, i. e. Romanesque, style by Albert Schmidt.

Even Ancient Greece is reflected in Munich's appearance. It was no less an art-fanatic than King Ludwig I that helped his capital to be labelled "Athens on the Isar", and the way he had the Königsplatz ('King's Square') laid out was instrumental in this. The preoccupation with Hellas was no coincidence. It did not only fit in with the spirit of the times but also with the family history of the Wittelsbachs. After all, Ludwig's son Otto was King of Greece from 1832 to 1862. Thus homage to Greece also finds its expression in the sculptures to be seen beneath the gable of the Propylaea.

The mighty entrance gate on the west side of Königsplatz is constructed out of marble from the Untersberg Mountain near Salzburg. It has been described as "a building of sublime uselessness" and combines Greek styles of building with motifs taken from Egyptian culture. The real model was the Propylaea of the Acropolis in Athens, of course. The nearby Glyptothek, built in the classical style with a portico of Ionic columns, also exudes the atmosphere of the ancient world.

Since 1980 the State Gallery of Modern Art has had its home in the west wing of the Haus der Kunst art gallery. On display are paintings and sculpture from the time of the expressionists up to the present.

This monumental edifice completed by Paul Ludwig Troost in 1937 dominates the Prinzregentenstrasse along with the Schack Gallery and the Prince Regent's Theatre. Since 1949, the annual "Main Art Exhibition of Munich" has been held here. In the last few decades the management of the gallery has succeeded in putting on exhibitions that have gained an international reputation by honouring the works of great European artists. In addition, the Haus der Kunst won a name for itself by showing treasures of Ancient Egypt such as "Nofretete the Beautiful". Starting out from Munich, this important exhibition was then sent on tour through Europe and to America and Japan. Here, too, the art treasures and life style of a Japanese prince of the Shogun era were first shown in Europe.

There have been well-patronized special displays of works by Picasso, Cézanne, Kandinsky, Chagall, Kokoschka, not forgetting the great "Max Beckmann Retrospective Exhibition" of 1984 and the exhibition entitled "In the Light of Claude Lorrain: Landscape Painting from Three Centuries".

The Bavarian State Chancellor's Office, former Army museum

The Propylaea, erected between 1846 and 1862 in the classical style

overleaf, left: The Angel of Peace on Prince Regent Bridge, erected by Heinrich Düll 1895–1899 based on Roman examples

overleaf, right: A circular mosaic on a gold background, from the Korenhalle, the foot of the monument

Semi-classical building by Klenze, the "Glyptothek"

"Prinz-Carl-Palais", former seat of the aristocracy

The art gallery – there are regular exhibitions here to show famous collections and special aspects of art

The Present-day Economy and Technology – the German Museum

The branches of industry that go to make up Munich's economy are varied and the companies are of different sizes. Certain conditions appeared essential for the establishment of large industries when they were being founded a century ago. It has now proved a blessing that those conditions were completely missing here. While the regions in which heavy industry once dominated – those regions that were the mainstay of the economy – are almost all struggling through crises, Munich is profiting from its infrastructure and image. There are even international concerns that would think exclusively of Munich when it came to choosing a location in Europe.

The good reputation of the Bavarian capital is due in no small way to its being an important centre for trade fairs. Every year over 2 million visitors from all four corners of the earth come to such fairs held at a special site in Munich, and the proportion of foreigners that come is about 20 per cent. Clearly Munich offers optimal conditions for successful trade fairs on account of its geographical situation, access by public and private transport and other infrastructural advantages. In addition, it can offer as many as 26,000 beds in over 400 hotels as well as numerous sights in the fields of art and culture that can be included to make up an excellent itinerary in connection with trade fairs and congresses. On top of this, one should not forget the typical flair of Munich.

A glance at the calendar of events reveals a considerable range of trade fairs. The organizers are convinced that concentrations such as those represented by electronics, the building industry or leisure and fashion meet a general demand. The best-known fairs are the International Fair for Sports Goods (ISPO), the International Congress for Dietetics (IKOFA), the International Hotels and Catering Fair (IGAFA), the International Building Fair (Interbau), the International Fair for the Construction Industry (BAUMA), the Caravan and Boat Exhibition including the International Travel Fair, the Munich Week of Fashion and, of course, the International Crafts Fair. In all, about 23,000 exhibitors take part in fairs here.

The economic strength of the Munich area itself has also attracted international attention in recent years. Following on from a centuries-old tradition in the crafts, in the first decades of this century many renowned companies in the fields of precision engineering, optics and electronics sprang up. This soon led to remarkable achievements in the construction of machines, vehicles and motor engines. Research and development have come to play an important part, as is the case in aeronautics, for example. Well-known firms representing the clothing, chemicals and paper-processing industries are to be found here, as are all the large banks and insurance companies. The claim that Munich is increasingly becoming a centre of the service sector is justified.

Beer is also an important factor in this city on the Isar, not only as liquid nourishment but also as a commodity. Munich is equally important as a distribution centre for agricultural goods, while the crafts also make an important contribution to local trade.

Business and technology would not be able to function without an effective transport system, and the Olympic Year of '72 saw the inauguration of the Combined Munich Transport Services (MVV)

right: Aircraft being filled with fuel at Munich Airport

People can easily get around in Munich thanks to local public transport provided by the Underground ("U-Bahn"), the Rapid Transit Railway ("S-Bahn") and trams

The Music Room in the German Museum

with their Go-As-You-Please tickets, thus setting the signal at green for a better journey into the future on Munich's public transport.

Up to this point in the book, the most famous museum in the city has only been touched upon: the "German Museum of Scientific and Technological Masterpieces". In 1903, when Oskar von Miller succeeded in founding a "German Society" whose aim was to establish a museum he could not have imagined the enthusiasm that the project was to arouse. Nowadays a million and a half people a year fall for the fascination of science and technology at the German Museum and are clearly unaffected by the scepticism with which these fields are regarded, in our times. Perhaps there is no longer euphoria at technological or scientific progress, but at least enormous interest in scientific advance has remained.

The thoughts that Max Planck entrusted the project with when opening the new building on Museum Island in 1925 hold true today: they stress that the interaction of science and technology is important for culture in general. The concept of the German Museum — a public institution financed in the main by the State of Bavaria, but also by the state capital Munich and the Federal

The German Museum, the largest museum of technology in the world

Government — has been retained. Its purpose is to help people to come to terms with the present state of technology and the way it determines our lives. This understanding can only be achieved through knowledge of the early stages and historical developments in science, which are here demonstrated by means of original apparatus and numerous working machines and models, as well as mock-ups of places of work. In addition there is a reference library with 700,000 volumes on its shelves.

The newly-organized section "Air and Space Travel", which was opened on 6th May, 1984, is proving to be a special attraction. The display area, which amounts to about 60,000 sq. feet, allows a unique comparison of flying machines from the very beginnings to the present day. This new hall and the extensive archives thus enshrine Germany's contibution to the history of aeronautics and space travel and they have become a mecca for those interested in this subject. There are about 1,000 exhibits, including 50 original items, many of which are of unrivalled historical importance. There are also special sections devoted, for example, to gliding, air traffic control and the broad field of construction and materials in aeronautics.

The Magdeburg Hemisphere, original dating back to 1663

Developments in the field of aviation and aeronautics

A Moorish dancer,
to be seen in the
Stadtmuseum ('City Museum')

Munich's Museums –
a Home
of the Arts

"Nobody really knows Germany until he or she has seen Munich." It was King Ludwig I who set his mind on turning his capital into <u>the</u> art metropolis of the 19th century. And he succeeded. His ambitious building schemes undoubtedly created the basis for Munich to become a city of museums.

The museums of Munich contribute to the city's individuality as well as being a reminder of the Wittelsbachs. This is made especially clear by the Municipal Gallery in the Lenbach House and by the City Museum.

The crowning glory of the exhibits in the City Museum, which is housed in the former mediaeval armory and granary, is a group of Moorish dancers. These statuettes, which are over 500 years old, used to adorn the ballroom in the Old City Hall. In the same house

one can admire a museum of puppet theatres, a section on travelling fairs and a display of musical instruments. In addition, a museum of photography and film is to be found here.

We owe the unique atmosphere that surrounds the collection of paintings by the group of Munich artists known as "Der blaue Reiter" (Kandinsky, Franz Marc, Gabriele Münter and August Macke) to the famous portrait painter of that period, Franz von Lenbach. The Municipal Gallery is housed in the former residence of that artist near Königsplatz. It was built in the style of an Italian Renaissance villa.

One of the finest museums in Munich is the Bavarian National Museum. Its attractions range from the beautiful exhibition rooms themselves to the exhibits, sculptures and objets d'art dating from the early Middle Ages down to the present century. The main attractions are the "Madonna With Rose Bush" sculpted in stone (c. 1320), the Flemish tapistry from the famous workshops of Brussels and wood carvings by Tilman Riemenschneider. In spite of its

Heinrich Campendock's
"Woman Playing the Shawm"
in the Municipal Gallery
in the Lenbach House

being nominally a "Bavarian" musem, the exhibits do not only originate from Bavaria. Also in the museum's possession are the famous model of the City of Munich made by the turner Jakob Sandtner as well as collections of porcelain, paintings on glass, carvings in ivory and beautiful marquetry. The range extends to folk art and a collection of Bavarian, Austrian and Italian cribs.

The plans for the construction of the National Museum were drawn up by Gabriel von Seidl and its conception reflects the personal influence of King Max II, who ordered the museum to be built. His objectives were educational rather than scientific or academic since he wished to demonstrate to the population at that time (1855) how productive and artistic the craftsmen of earlier eras had been by putting examples of their work on display. The varied architectural style of this group of buildings prepares the visitor for what awaits him inside: art of various eras from the early Middle Ages down to our day.

The National Museum:
an important collection of Bavarian art treasures

"Hunting the Unicorn"
as shown on the fragment
of a tapistry from
Franconia (c. 1450)

The showpiece of the National Museum: "St. Mary Magdalene Being Raised to Heaven by Angels" by Tilmann Riemenschneider

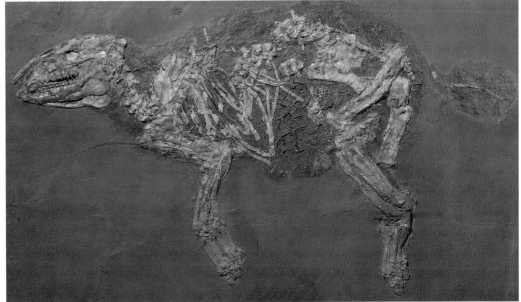

Museum "Man and Nature"; a glance into the department "History of Life"

The state collection of prehistoric remains in the Museum of Prehistoric and Early History was initiated in 1885. In 1977 the collection was moved into a new museum building where archaeological remains from the Early Stone Age (c. 100,000 B. C.) down to the Early Middle Ages and the Carolingian era (9th - 10th century A. D.) are on permanent display. The exhibition is supplemented by finds from the Middle Ages made within the bounds of Munich. Models, drawings and photographs of excavations illustrate to visitors the different types of settlement, burial customs, dress and craftsmanship from the Stone Age, through the Bronze Age, the Celtic culture and the Roman era, down to the Early Middle Ages. Special exhibitions are put on in order to show parts of the large stock of items from the Near East. This museum also provides conducted tours for school parties and a programme especially for the blind.

Protection for a horse's head during tournaments and parades — found at Eining (Roman: early 3rd cent. A. D.)

The statuette of a horse, fashioned in dark brown clay — found in a grave of the Hallstatt Age near Prächting (7th cent. B. C.)

A stirrup clasp of silver gilt found in the grave of a rich woman at Wittislingen (7th cent. A. D.)

The Old Pinacothek with its collections of European painting from the 14th to 18th centuries is one of the most important art galleries in the world. The main stress is on 15th- and 16th-century painting from Germany and the Low Countries, Dutch and Flemish paintings of the 17th century, Italian paintings of the 15th to 18th centuries and French and Spanish baroque painting.

The passion for collecting that was shared by the many branches of the Wittelsbach family provided the basis of the collections. The cycle of historical paintings commissioned by Wilhelm IV in the years 1528 – 40, from which the so-called "Battle of Alexander" by Altdorfer originates, constitutes the "original seed" of the collections. Maximilian I (ruled 1597 – 1651) directed his attention to the works of Dürer and acquired the "Four Apostles" and the "Paumgartner Altar" for his "Cammer-Galleria" in the Residence. Max

The "Lenbachhaus", artists' residence

Peter Paul Rubens: "The Lion Hunt"

Emanuel (ruled 1679 – 1726), who built the New Palace at Schleissheim, added Italian and French baroque paintings, and, with the Gisbert van Colen collection, works by Rubens, van Dyck, Brouwer and Jan Brueghel among others.

The merging of the Wittelsbach collections in Düsseldorf, Mannheim and Zweibrücken with the Electoral Gallery in Munich in the years around 1800 together with the acquisition of church treasures that passed to the state as a result of secularization after 1803 meant an enormous expansion. At the same time the collection received a new function in addition to that of creating personal prestige for the dukes and elektors: during the Enlightenment it was used as an instrument of popular education. Thus Karl Theodor (ruled 1777 – 99) was the first to allow access to the Elektoral Gallery — by an entrance on the northern side facing the Hofgarten ('Court Garden').

But it was Ludwig I (ruled 1821 – 48) and his architect Leo von Klenze who were to create an early example of real museum architecture with their construction of the Old Pinacothek (completed 1836). Of the scheme of idealistic and instructive statues and deco-rations little remains today, much having been destroyed by the bombs of World War II or altered by the programme of reconstruction (1957).

By purchasing individual works in Italy (Raffael's "Madonna Tempi", for example) and acquiring the Boisserée Collection (the Lower Rhine and Cologne School and early Dutch works like Rogier's "Altar of the Three Kings") Ludwig was able to give a new emphasis to the collection. Even today, paintings by French artists of the 18th century that have been acquired through the help of foundations bear witness to an active museum policy which continues to shape the Old Pinacothek.

Rogier van der Weyden: "The Adoration of the Magi" on the Altar of the Three Kings or Columba Altar (c. 1455) in the Old Pinacothek

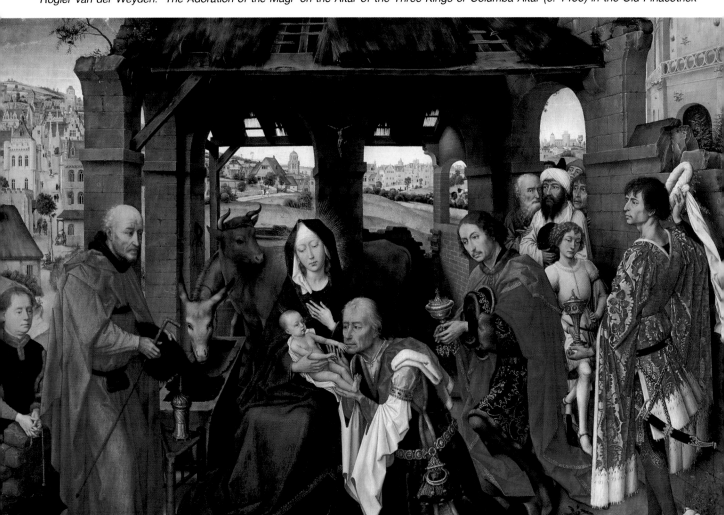

On the site of the New Pinacothek, which was opened in 1981, there stood the original museum designed by August von Voits and commissioned by Ludwig I for the purpose of exhibiting contemporary art. It had been built between 1846 and 1853 and was destroyed in 1944 – 45.

Nowadays, a selection of about 600 paintings and sculptures dating from the late 18th to early 20th centuries are on show here, and the main focus is on paintings collected by Ludwig I (German Classicism, Nazarenes and Munich School) and donations such as those by C. Fiedler (works by Marées), or the so-called "Tschude Donation" (French impressionists, Gauguin, van Gogh).

The south face of the New Pinacothek with a sculpture by Henry Moore

Carl Spitzweg, 1808–1885: "A Visit from the Father of the People"

An exhibition room in the New Pinacothek

Munich's Theatres and Concert Halls

In the field of drama, city and state have split their responsibilities, while the realm of music has remained entirely in the hands of the state. Operas, operettas and musicals are presented on the stages of the National Theatre, the Cuvilliés Theatre and the Theatre at Gärtnerplatz. Drama is at home on the stages of the state-run Residence Theatre and municipal Kammerspiele ('Studio Theatres') as well as in numerous privately-owned playhouses.

Carl von Fischer was the name of the master builder who in the years 1811 to 1818 was commissioned by the first King of Bavaria, Max Joseph, to design a new national and court theatre. However, it burnt down in the year 1823, and Leo von Klenze supervised the

A scene from Richard Strauss's "Rosenkavalier"

reconstruction from the old plans, but with minimal alterations. The highest gable with its decoration in mosaic, for example, originates from von Klenze.

It was here that Richard Wagner in particular celebrated his greatest triumphs. "Tristan and Isolde", "The Mastersingers of Nuremberg", "Rhinegold" and "The Valkyries" had their premieres in the National Theatre. In the Second World War it was gutted once again and was subsequently rebuilt. The construction of the present-day National Theatre was financed by donations from the citizens of Munich. The inauguration took place on 21st November, 1963 with a gala performance of "The Mastersingers". From that date onwards, the theatre has not only consistently presented truly great festivals of music. Since its opening it has also silenced those critics

The Cuvilliés Theatre, 1751–1753

The National Theatre
at Max Joseph Square:
its truly great festivals
of music attract opera-lovers
from all over the world
just as much now as at the
inauguration in 1818

An open-air performance at the Old Mint

Munich's most famous concert hall: the Hercules Hall in the Residence

who would have risked an experiment rather than carefully constructing a replica of the building designed by Carl von Fischer.

Five years previously, everyone had been impressed by the skill with which the Old Residence Theatre had been brought back to life in the course of restoration work on the Residence itself. Thanks to some far-sighted men who had promptly removed the unique rococo interior and thus saved it from destruction, the playhouse also called the Cuvilliés Theatre, which had been totally destroyed in the War, became one of the gems of Munich once again. The re-opening with "The Marriage of Figaro" was at least as brilliant as that evening in this theatre when the 25-year-old Mozart presented his "Idomeneo" for the first time.

It is the spoken word that dominates in the New Residence Theatre, which was originally reserved for classical drama. In contrast, the Municipal Playhouses, including the various studio theatres such as the Werkraumtheater ('Theatre in the Workshop'), provide a stage that is intended to be the preserve of modern authors.
64

However, this distinction no longer holds true. Works from a whole range of periods have found their way into both types of theatre.

The inhabitant of Munich and his guests can enjoy operatic performances not only at the National Theatre but also in the courtyard of the old Mint Office, where an encounter with a Mozart opera on the open-air stage may certainly be considered one of the most delightful experiences in Munich's summer cultural season. The Mint originated as a "chamber of art" in the years 1563 to 1567, when considerable alterations were being made to the Residence. That was the time of Albrecht V, and it saw the late mediaeval style of building give way to the Renaissance.

The "Gasteig" is Munich's cultural, educational and conference centre. The heart of the "Gasteig" is the philharmonia, home of the Munich Philharmonic

*The re-inaugurated
Prince Regents' Theatre*

All types of theatre are here:
a puppet theatre, cabaret
and street theatres

"Bavaria Film Studios at Geiselgasteig",
scenes from "Das Boot" and
"The Never-ending Story"

Without a doubt, the centre of concert life is now the Herkulessaal ('Hercules Hall') of the Residence. It was only built into the northern wing of the Residence, which contains halls for festive occasions, after the Second World War.

When one considers the whole range of cultural activities on the Isar that go under the heading "Theatre and Cabaret", it becomes clear that it stretches from the puppet theatre to the State Opera. And marionettes play by no means a minor role. The City Museum houses not only the largest collection of items in the world from puppet theatres but also a performing puppet theatre, which is renowned for its productions with spoken dialogue. It concentrates mainly on fairy tales, but successful attempts have also been made at opera from Mozart to Carl Orff. Thus not only the youngsters of Munich, who love their puppet theatre for its performances of fairy tales, but also the grown-ups of the city have been filled with enthusiasm. The numbers of visitors already bear testimony to this. Cabaret is, of course, still the preserve of Schwabing, even if other districts are beginning to offer similar entertainment. The studio theatres with imaginative names like "TamS" or "Off-Off" continually attract attention and demonstrate that, apart from the state theatres and the famous private ones — from Das Deutsche Theater down to the Kleine Freiheit (roughly 'Little Liberties') — there are countless small ones that risk a performance every evening, even without the security of a state subsidy. And there are even artists that do not wait for their audience to appear — the idealists of the street theatre.

Schwabing – a Very Special District

Schwabing is certainly no longer what it was. Neither the customary moaning nor nostalgic grumbling are concealed behind this deep sigh of regret, but rather the admission that the bohemian quarter Schwabing that became famous throughout Europe a century ago no longer exists. Geographically speaking, Schwabing was considered to be merely one of the villages on the northern outskirts of the city. But nowadays it is not only the whole district north of Theresienstrasse that basks in the glamour of this name. As a result of commercialization the definition of Schwabing goes beyond these bounds.

Earlier, typical inns of Schwabing such as "Simplicissimus" owed their atmosphere to celebrities like Wedekind or Heinrich Mann, who lived in Munich for a time. By way of contrast, the present-day influence of immigrants from North Germany can hardly be called novel.

As this change took its course, artists were driven out of their studios and students out of their cheap flats. Thus the uniqueness of this typical quarter of Munich was lost and replaced by a commonplace atmosphere. Only a warm summer evening in Leopoldstrasse and its vicinities can give any idea of the past that is gone for ever.

Without the countless theatres in cellars and back-yards working on insufficient budgets to present avant-garde productions one would hardly be able to detect the flair of this district which became part of Munich as a result of local government reform in 1891 and which almost succeeded in eclipsing the popularity of the state capital itself, at least in the eyes of most outsiders. The famous say-

Schwabing, the home of artists or
a place where people just stroll about in order
to see other people or be seen themselves

The work of sculptors, painters and other artists, whether in private or in public, dominates the life of Schwabing

ing by Countess Reventlow that Schwabing is not a place but a state of mind is generally taken quite ironically nowadays: "The inhabitants of Schwabing really are in quite a state …".

The Victory Arch is the bottleneck that the citizens of Munich have to pass in order to reach "their" Schwabing — at least coming from the city centre. Karl Valentin once made the profound remark that Victory Arch is "open night and day." And this is especially true of our times. Leopoldstrasse, which is lined on both sides by poplars, starts at Victory Arch; before it, the boulevard past the University is called Ludwigstrasse and is the main thoroughfare for the incessant streams of traffic to and from Schwabing. As already mentioned, the definition of what is Schwabing is by no means a narrow one, so that the surrounding streets where, for example, the Academy of Fine Arts is situated are also considered to be part of the district. In fact, there is no hesitation when it comes to incorporating the whole of the Max-Vorstadt ('Max Suburban District'). These streets and alleys, which strictly speaking do not belong to the district, help to make Schwabing really Babylonian and worthy of its nickname "Schwabylon". In this connection some might mention Türkenstrasse ('Turk Street') where the "Eleven Executioners" once

did their duties, or where Kathi Kobus founded her "Simplicissimus". The latter survives as the Alter Simpl but is unable to conceal the fact that things have changed a lot here as has the whole scene in Schwabing. After the Second World War there were some hopeful signs that Old Schwabing might be re-born, but they have come to practically nothing.

The Victory Arch dates from the middle of the last century. Friedrich von Gärtner drew up the plans with the Constantine Arch in Rome serving him as a model. The arch is surmounted by Bavaria steering a chariot being drawn away from the city by four lions. Johann Martin von Wagner originally created this group, which was resculpted by Elmar Dietz after it had been severely damaged in the Second World War.

The Victory Arch commemorating the defeat of Napoleon I.
At the end of the wide boulevard there is the Hall of the Generals

The University

Munich has not been a university town for very long. It was only in 1826 that King Ludwig I decreed that the University should be transferred to Munich. It had been founded at Ingolstadt in 1472 and had been moved to Landshut in 1802. The University, which was housed in the illustrious Ludwigstrasse in buildings considered at the time to be well-equipped, soon grew in importance, particularly under the influence of the North Germans appointed by King Max II. The teaching staff were frequently made fun of and lampooned as "Non-Bavarians" and "Non-Catholics". Even so, together with local scholars they soon managed to get the University of Munich a reputation for high academic standards. This holds especially true for the sciences and has been underlined by the fact that a number of Munich professors have received the Nobel Prize. In recent years the University has burst at the seams and spread out into other districts.

The main buildings of the Ludwig-Maximilians-Universität were designed by Friedrich von Gärtner, which explains the harmony that may be detected between them and St. Ludwig's Church (built 1829 – 44). The square in front of the University is dedicated to the Scholls, a brother and sister that together with their professor Kurt Huber were executed by the Hitler regime.

Maximilianstrasse, which leads away from Max-Joseph Square, may well be impressive, but what stands at the end of it is truly monumental: the Maximilianeum. This building with arcades, which towers majestically above the Isar, once housed a training

Ludwigstrasse with the University Fountain and a view of the Ludwig's Church

The Ludwig-Maximilian University, commissioned
by King Ludwig I and built between 1835 and 1840

college for cadets and is now the home of the Landtag, the parliament of the Free State of Bavaria.

It is interesting to note that Maximilianeum can mean three things. First and foremost, it is the building which was begun in 1857 and completed in 1874. Secondly, the term Maximilianeum is used as the title of an academic foundation called into being by King Max II that enables highly gifted university entrants to study free of all financial worries. These students live in the Maximilianeum itself.

The Maximilianeum

The Light-hearted Side of Munich

The citizens of Munich have grown fond of their trams, but of other things too: the Auer Dult ('Mart at Au'), for example, which some people even consider to be more typical of Munich than the October Festival. For over two centuries — since the time of the elector Theodor — stalls have been put up three times a year in this suburb. The magic of this little fair ranges from the smell of roasting chestnuts to the surprise bargains at the junk stalls. The people of Munich in fact prefer to celebrate in a modest way — but all the more often. So there are fairs to be found somewhere in the region all the year round.

Some things about the Wies'n ('[Fair in the] Meads'), as the people from Munich and elsewhere call the world-famous October Festival, are rather contradictory. Everyone has now got used to the fact that the world's greatest fair begins in September and only lasts into October by a few days at the most. Hardly anyone is kept away by the perennial discussion about the October Festival being daylight robbery or by those that complain that it is not what it was. Of course, never a year passes without the topic of short measure cropping up, and this sometimes even gives the legal profession a

Two aspects of the city's tradition that are very popular with the people of Munich: the trams and the Auer Dult ('Mart at Au')

little extra work. But, when things really get going, there the moaners are again, planted behind their freshly-filled litre mugs or swilling down their grumpiness by the mouthful, all simply glad to be living in Munich and nowhere else …

The October Festival at the Theresienwiese ('St. Teresa's Meadow'), which is one of the world's largest fairs, has two focal points: the Central Agricultural Show and the big parade of people in traditional costumes

It all began in 1810, when the citizens of Munich wanted to make their contribution to the festivities on the occasion of Crown Prince Ludwig's wedding to Princess Therese of Saxony-Hildburghausen. The commoner and hackney carriage driver Franz Baumgartner and a major in the National Guard by the name of Andreas Dall'Armi recalled an ancient tradition and organized a horse race for that day. This event was the focal point of the festival until well past the middle of the 19th century. But soon all the other attractions of a real fair, which not only in Munich are considered to be typical of the October Festival, came to be associated with it. Around the world there are said to be 200 "October Festivals", but not one of them has yet succeeded in eclipsing the popularity of the Wies'n at Munich.

Even if the artists' parties and balls in Schwabing are not what they were, Fasching still means a lot of fun for the people of Munich. Here on the Isar, neither carnival speeches (some witty, others less so) nor lavish parades are a mark of the fifth season of the year, as they are on the Rhine. Instead, in Munich the black-and-white society balls and the light-hearted fancy-dress parties that cannot even be spoilt by the long faces of the professional moaners are the order of the day.

One would of course be exaggerating if one were to assume that the typical inhabitant of Munich impatiently awaits "the days of bedlam, when he is ready to let it rip," as Otto Hiebl, head of the city's tourist services, once put it. Being a melancholic, he is more likely to keep asking himself and others what is really so special about Fasching and to indulge in nostalgic memories of the riotous "good old days" of the past. And so he keeps on grumbling until Fasching comes round again and it is time for him to plunge into all the dances. When he gets to the cloakroom, he moans to the attendant that everything used to be better — and cheaper. "When we were young, the people themselves were at the centre of things, and there was no need for professional jokers, and ..., well, you know what I mean."

What may be considered typical of Fasching in Munich is the variety of novel, droll, crazy or simply run-of-the-mill dances. A speciality of a rather unusual kind is certainly to be found in the "Night

It would be true to say that the Bavarians have never thought much of organized jollity. In spite of the increasing risks of Munich being swamped by foreigners moving in from other parts of Germany, this attitude may be considered typical of the genuine Bavarian. One could even go further and say that Munich's power to assimilate new arrivals makes the "Prussians" (the Bavarian term for all non-Bavarians) more typical of Munich than the natives themselves after a short time. This phenomenon may especially be noticed in Fasching.

of the Zany Knights", the seething celebrations in the Haus der Kunst, or the balls that have the Olympic Hall as their impressive setting. "Black-and-white dances" are by no means synonymous with "stiff boredom". In any case, the inhabitant of Munich does not think it is necessary to put on fancy dress in order to have a merry time. On the other hand, whether hiding behind a mask or not, he is not slow to make fun of himself. Even in Fasching, the people of Munich remain true to their maxim: live and let live.

The citizen of Munich takes to the streets when he feels like it, and that happens particularly on the last Sunday in Fasching when the whole city "goes crazy". On the last Tuesday in Fasching (Shrove Tuesday), the women stallholders at the Viktualienmarkt do their best to add to the atmosphere, and give the Munich Fasching a rather coarse flavour with their earthy humour. As far as celebrating is concerned, in modern times the people of Munich still adhere to age-old customs.

Carnival in Munich implies the "stupid knights" and their famous ball, the market-women at the open-air food-market, people milling on the streets, and fun in the colourfully decorated halls

The Olympic Park in Munich – Always Worth a Visit

What nobody thought could happen after the Olympics of 1972 has come true: the Olympic Park has turned into one of the lasting attractions in Munich. It has even become a symbol of the city. Every day visitors from all four corners of the world flock to Europe's largest leisure park and recreation area. Millions of people pay entry for sporting and other events, while others just come to relax and walk around the fine grounds. The olympic sports facilities form a complex which is still unique in the whole world. It is the 950-

View of the nearby BMW Tower from the Olympic Park

foot Olympic Tower and the tent-like roof over the stadium that dominate the scene, but what really gives the place its magic touch is the fascinating architecture set in a hilly and varied landscape, all created by human hand.

Since the Olympics, these facilities have been the setting for literally thousands of sporting, cultural and commercial functions, and the great number of mammoth events helps to keep the Olympic Park in the limelight. But this is only one aspect of the Park. The Olympic Grounds are a perfect recreation area for the people of Munich and a tourist attraction for visitors from other places. Here people will always discover anew the combination of unique architecture and beautiful landscape, all within easy reach of Munich's city centre.

The bold architecture and lay-out of the sports facilities for the 1972 Olympics, still in great demand today as a leisure area and for great sporting occasions

Leafy Munich

One of the reasons why Munich has retained its attraction is that it has kept its areas of green despite enormous expansion. The embankments and parks that stretch from south to north along the Isar through the city help to give Munich its special atmosphere. In fact, one can pass from the zoo at Hellabrunn to Unterföhring and beyond right in the north without leaving tree-lined walks.

The people of Munich have exploited this wealth of greenery in their own manner. Throughout this "international metropolis with a warm heart" you can find beer gardens, some of which can look back on a long tradition. Here the people of Munich like to relax on the hot days or in the mild evenings of summer. And the beer gardens are by no means an exclusively male preserve. When you go to one for a break and something to eat and order a litre of fresh beer from the waiter or waitress, you are sure to be involved in a friendly chat with other customers before long.

The English Garden is not only important as an enormous "green lung" for the city, but also a park for leisure and relaxation, and its origins are even of historical interest. The elector Karl Theodor was persuaded by Count von Rumford to create a type of landscape garden that was revolutionary for the time. Instead of disciplining Nature into geometrical forms, as had been done in rococo-style gardens, the landscape gardeners ceased to give Nature a short back and sides. Friedrich Ludwig von Sekell, the creator of the English Garden, preferred free growth and wide open spaces.

From 1790 onwards, the first German public park with free access was laid out here on a rather marshy site that had originally been the Wittelsbachs' hunting grounds. The English Garden stretches for over three miles from the art gallery Haus der Kunst to Aumeister, a popular inn. While a landscape consisting mainly of river meads has been preserved in the north of the garden, the variation between meadows, copses and rather unusual buildings in the southern part reminds us that a landscape gardener was in fact trying to form Nature here.

Two things to be enjoyed in a Munich beer garden: the world-famous Munich beer and the Bavarian manner of taking things easy

What would Munich be without the English Garden? You can walk or cycle for hours on end in this, the first public park in Germany. Here you can climb up to the Monopteros Temple, perched invitingly at the top of a small rise, or you can still your hunger in the shade of the Pagoda

An autumn day near the Isar river

The most important buildings in the English Garden are worthy of note. On an island in the middle of a lake there is a Japanese tea house where genuine Japanese tea ceremonies often take place.

From the Monopteros, a small round temple at the top of a hillock, a particularly fine view is to be had over the city. The Pagoda was destroyed in the last war but then rebuilt in its elegant style so that it has lost none of its attractiveness.

Of the first Botanical Garden in Munich, which was opened in 1812, only a small part remains: the Old Botanical Garden, located on the north side of the Palace of Justice, not far from the Central Railway Station. It is now a small municipal park with the Neptune Fountain at its centre, and no longer a real botanical garden.

The present-day Botanical Garden has been situated since 1914 in Nymphenburg, where it borders on the north side of the palace grounds. It is not only an important academy where Botany is taught and research is done but also an institution that furnishes all interested visitors with knowledge of plants and biology. Furthermore, young and old may enjoy relaxing hours in a floral splendour that changes from season to season in beautifully laid-out gardens.

This is one of the finest botanical gardens in Europe, and indeed the whole world. The great variety of open beds — the ornamental garden, the parkland (arboretum), the heather garden, the alpine rockery, the valley of ferns or the rhododendron garden, for example, as well as the valuable collections of exotic plants such as tropical orchids, palms, giant bamboos, insect-eating plants, tropical water plants, cacti, other succulents and stag's horn ferns, to name but a few, enjoy an international reputation.

The West Park, which was the site of the IGA (International Horticultural Show) in 1983, has been turned into a valuable recreation area. The main feature of the park is a broad, open valley with gently sloping sides, vantage points, lakes and streams, all modelled on the moraine landscape to be found in the foothills of the Alps.

The Botanical Garden close
by Nymphenburg Palace

Various features and facilities such as a rose garden, beds of flowering shrubs, restaurants, beer gardens, play areas and other attractions are set in this park and are connected by spacious walks.

And then there is the Isar. The people of Munich refer to the river as "the raging torrent", but nowadays it only rarely lives up to this description. Nevertheless, the river is still good for an amusing trip on a raft, even if the current has been tamed by engineers. It is no wonder that such frolics — accompanied by the inevitable beer and music — are one of the most popular summer pastimes for both locals and visitors. During the five-hour trip from Wolfratshausen to the Thalkirchen district of Munich there is ample opportunity to take a dip in the water, enjoy a cold snack and have a good look at the meadows along the Isar. A trip on a raft is, however, not the only attraction that Munich's surroundings hold in store. In fact the city is in the middle of such beautiful scenery that one is spoilt for choice when trying to decide on a place for a trip out. To the north-west there are the hills by Dachau; there are dense, inviting forests to the east, or the plateau with its lakes to the south. Finally, there is the chain of the Alps on the distant horizon, popular with climbers and walkers in summer and skiers in winter, especially at the weekends when hundreds of thousands make their way to the mountains.

And not to forget the gems of "Old Bavaria", King Ludwig's castles: Neuschwanstein, Linderhof and Herrenchiemsee. They are always worth a visit, which is of course true of the whole of Upper Bavaria with its rolling hills and baroque onion spires. Bavaria, mountains and baroque are simply words that go together!

Over the years Hellabrunn Zoo, which is set in the valley of the Isar has become one of the largest and certainly one of the finest zoological gardens in Europe. Its beginnings were not without problems, however. The gardens were inaugurated by Emanuel von Seidl in 1911, but had to be closed as a result of the inflation after the First World War. Heinz Heck managed to have them reopened, and set

The grounds of the International Horticultural Show (IGA 1983), now known as the West Park

Fun on the water: a raft trip or surfing on the rapids of the fast-flowing Isar

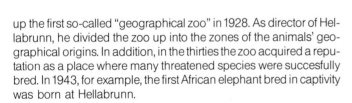

up the first so-called "geographical zoo" in 1928. As director of Hellabrunn, he divided the zoo up into the zones of the animals' geographical origins. In addition, in the thirties the zoo acquired a reputation as a place where many threatened species were succesfully bred. In 1943, for example, the first African elephant bred in captivity was born at Hellabrunn.

After the zoo had ventured a fresh start for the third time after the severe damage of World War II, a completely new arrangement was begun in the seventies. Nowadays, for example, there is no fence to disrupt one's view of the elephants; it has given way to a narrow trench. In the famous ape house the bars have been replaced by glass. The snakes and crocodiles are now kept in a modern terrarium, and the aquarium has been completely renovated. The enclosures for the zebras, antilopes and ostriches resemble a miniature Serengeti. The "polarium" with its seals, sea-lions and sea-elephants is a special attraction. On top of all these features there are the children's zoo and a play area, all intended to make a visit to Hellabrunn the perfect family outing.

Hellabrunn also has something special for the very young: a children's zoo where animals may be picked up and stroked and a play area

One of the attractions in Hellabrunn Zoo is the elephant house

Palaces, Castles and Places of Pilgrimage

Nymphenburg, Amalienburg, Blutenburg and finally Schleissheim Palace — the list is incomplete, but it gives a fairly good impression of what Munich's environs have to offer since it is not only the city itself that is worth seeing. To the west, the residential areas long ago relentlessly spread out and surrounded those open fields on which the elector Max Emanuel extended his mother's modest country villa to make it into a magnificent palace and grounds. Taking a first look at Nymphenburg, one notes the avenue and canal leading up to the palace directly from the east. The focal point is the cube-shaped construction in the centre, built for the electress Henriette Adelaide by Agostino Barelli in the years after 1664. A double open stairway leads up to its entrance. Josef Effner was responsible for the alteration works on the facade of the central section, which has single-storey wings connecting it on either side to elegant villas.

Nymphenburg Palace: it took over 50 years to build this architectural gem

The interior of Nymphenburg Palace was originally dominated by the Hall of Stone, which owes its present appearance to Cuvilliés the Elder, while much of its vitality is due to the stucco decoration and frescoes by Johann Baptist Zimmerman. But the Chinese Room is also worth a special mention, as is the "Gallery of Beauties", painted by the court artist Joseph Stieler for King Ludwig I.

Here there are 36 portraits of the most beautiful women from all the social classes of Munich. This gallery ranges from Ludwig II's mother, Queen Marie of Bavaria, to the cobbler's daughter Helene Sedlmayr and the dancer Lola Montez, whose liaison with Ludwig I caused the sixty-year-old king to give up his claim to the throne. While the interior of Nymphenburg Palace is much less elaborately decorated than, for example, Schleissheim Palace, it is the park that is so impressive with its white marble figures and its lodges. Without a doubt, the Amalienburg hunting lodge with its circular hall of mirrors represents the climax of rococo creation. Here, François Cuvilliés even succeeded in emulating the French examples of this style.

A most unusual feature of the Badenburg lodge is Max Emanuel's heated baroque baths, while the Pagodenburg is a prime specimen of an old courtly summer residence.

To the north-west of Munich there is the unique Blutenburg Castle,

In winter its canal is often used as a skating rink

King Ludwig I's "Gallery of Beauties" at Nymphenburg Palace, where the parks leave an impression of fine harmony

Tucked away in the palace gardens are pleasant surprises such as the Amalienburg, the hunting lodge that the electress Maria Amalie had built in the years 1734 – 1739

a real jewel that was first mentioned in 1432. The main attraction here is the wood carvings along the walls of the chapel, which was built in 1488 by the same Duke Sigismund who laid the foundation stone for the Frauenkirche. Among the carvings is the so-called Blutenburg Madonna, created by an unknown master from Munich in the late 15th century.

A further sight in the immediate surroundings of Munich is Schleissheim Palace, which was completed at the beginning of the 18th century and is considered to be one of the most elaborate examples of European baroque. Enrico Zuccalli, whom Max Emanuel had made responsible for the construction work, drew up the original plans. The powerful 360-yard-long facade is particularly impressive, although the building is fairly squat and with little depth. Zuccalli's successor, Joseph Effner, who was born in Dachau, dispensed with the tower which, according to the original plans, was to have crowned the central section. Effner received his training in Paris and is regarded as the originator of Bavarian rococo, a style which came to flourish under his pupil, Cuvilliés, who was actually taken on by the court as chamberlain and dwarf. The interior of the palace is dominated by decoration glorifying Max Emanuel, vanquisher of the Turks, and the focal point is stucco-work by

Johann Baptist Zimmermann. But the baroque spirit can also be detected in the battle scenes painted by F. J. Reich and in a portrait on the ceiling originating from Amigoni's workshop. In some rooms of the palace one can find baroque paintings of Dutch or Flemish origin. The same is true of the lodge Lustheim, where one can also admire a collection of Meissen porcelain.

Blutenburg Castle, built as a hunting lodge in the years 1435 – 1438

*Grünwald Castle, now a museum housing
the state collections of prehistoric
remains and numerous archaeological finds*

Schleissheim Palace, built by the elector Max Emanuel in the years 1701–1704

Maria Ramersdorf is a fine example of the late Gothic pilgrimage church which is to be found throughout areas of original Bavarian settlement. The interior received its baroque decoration in 1675; the stucco-work was probably carried out by Wolfgang Zwenger the Younger of Schliersee.

Erasmus Grasser, a master of the late Gothic period, fashioned the statue of the madonna at the high altar, the focal point of the church. Under a priceless baldachin the Queen of Heaven sits holding the Holy Child. The most valuable treasure in the church is a relic donated by the son of Emperor Ludwig the Bavarian. The jewel is set in the imperial cross, which forms the centre-piece of a monstrance.

Bavarian devoutness finds its expression in the impressive numbers of churches in the towns and throughout the country, and the excellence of the master builders and artists has borne testimony to that religious feeling.

Churches such as those at Altötting, Ettal Abbey or the Wieskirche pilgrimage church (lit. 'Church in the Meadows') must here stand for the many.

The pilgrimage church Maria Ramersdorf

Lady Bavaria

"The Bavaria", which was cast in 1850 by Ferdinand von Miller using plans by Ludwig von Schwanthaler is about 50 feet high. Whether the model for this late offshoot of the Schwanthaler dynasty really was Schwanthaler's daughter cannot be determined. Nevertheless, it was certainly a young woman of Munich that caused Friedrich Hebbel to enthuse: "She is the very opposite of her husband: nobody can understand how she could marry him, and she certainly would not have done so if she had had any other choice." She personified the pulsating South, said the poet, with just a little ice and snow added. "Italian and German influences are struggling to win possession of her heart, which gives off sudden bursts of fiery passion and shows touching faithfulness — all at the same time!"

King Ludwig I may well have been a connoisseur when it came to women, but his main intention was to prove to the whole world what the city of Munich was capable of in the field of iron casting. He was hardly thinking of the psyche of Munich's women when, having looked to the Acropolis in Athens, he decided to erect a symbol of Bavarian and German strength. "The Bavaria" was supposed to develop the same symbolic power as the Athena Promachos, and together with her apparently tame lion, she has indeed come to e-pitomize the Bavarian way of life. This is not simply on account of the nearby October Festival, which takes place about one hundred feet below the statue towering on its massive base.

"The Bavaria" is embraced by the "U" of the Hall of Fame. Leo von Klenze was the builder of this open hall with its rows of Doric columns. In it, busts are displayed in honour of famous Bavarians. Attempts are being made to revive that tradition in the present day.

The Hall of Fame at the Theresienwiese

King Ludwig I stepped down two years before Ferdinand von Miller finished his work on "The Bavaria", which was certainly the greatest achievement by the clock-maker's son from Fürstenfeldbruck, who had taken over the Munich iron foundry after years as an apprentice and gaining experience in Paris and London. The casting work on the colossal figure took eight years, and about 86 tons of ore were used. One year after its completion, von Miller was awarded the gold medal at an international exhibition in London for his quadriga on the Victory Arch. At that time the demand from across the Atlantic for cast-iron statues was so great that von Miller was commissioned to produce an equestrian statue of Washington, a statue of Bolivar for Venezuela, and received other contracts. The bronze gates of the Capitol in Washington, for example, were produced in von Miller's workshops.

Thus the wheel completes its circle: Munich has always been a point of departure for famous personalities, but also a magnet to people from the North of Germany and other places. The new arrivals became integrated as citizens of Munich before they realized it, and that process is still going on today.

"The Bavaria" in front of the Hall of Fame   *overleaf: Mountains and lakes in Munich's beautiful surroundings*

Table of Contents

© Schmid Verlag GmbH Regensburg – Salzburg – Wien
Produktion: Schmid Verlag GmbH, Regensburg
Konzept/Gestaltung: Fachberatung Peter Stemmle, Regensburg
Texte: Gerd Otto, Regensburg
Übersetzer: Adrian Towersey, B. A.
Satz/Repro: Rotaplan Offset Kammann Druck GmbH
Druck: Aumüller Druck KG
Bindung: Conzella, Verlagsbuchbinderei, Pfarrkirchen
Bildnachweis:
Toni Angermayer: 85 u – Artothek: 58, 59, 61 – Augustiner Groß-
gaststätten: 32 r – Bavaria Filmtour: 66 m, 66 u – Bavaria Verlag:
16 l, 57 u – Bayerisches Nationalmuseum, München: 54 u –
Bayerische Verwaltung der staatlichen Schlösser, Gärten und
Seen: 17 – Fridmar Damm: Umschlag vorne, 7, 8, 10 (3x), 12,
20/21, 23, 28 r, 29 o, 31, 44 (2x), 45 (3x), 46, 48 lu, 50 u, 51 u,
54 o, 74 lm, 74 lu, 74 r, 78 o, 79 u, 80 r, 81 (3x) – Deutsches Museum, München: 50 o, 51 o – Bruno Dewald: 65 o – Flughafen
München GmbH (Dr. Werner Hennies): 49 – Fremdenverkehrsamt München (Bjarne Geiges): 22 o – Fremdenverkehrsamt

München (Dr. Jochen Müller): 6 – Fremdenverkehrsamt München
(Christl Reiter): 11 – Gasteig BetriebsgesmbH: 65 u – Bjarne
Geiges: 9 o, 25 u, 27 ro, 27 u (2x), 32 lu, 66 ro – Fotoverlag
Herpich: 87 u, 90 u – Robert Hetz: 5, 19, 25 lo, 26 u, 30 o,
35 r (2x), 36 l, 37 u, 38, 39 r, 39 lu, 40 o, 42 r (2x), 43 l, 48 ru,
60 u, 62 (2x), 63 o (2x), 64 (2x), 66 lo, 68 (3x), 73 o, 74 lo, 76 (2x),
77 (2x), 80 l, 84 (2x), 87 o, 88 o (2x), 92 – Hofbräuhaus: 33 r –
Joachim Kankel: 13, 14, 15 (2x), 16 r, 18, 24, 26 o, 28 lo, 28 lu,
29 u (2x), 36 r, 37 o, 40 u, 41 u, 43 r, 55 o, 69, 70, 72, 78 u, 82,
83, 86 (2x), 88 u, 89, 90 o, 91, 93 – Bildarchiv Reinhold Kirsch:
2/3, 94/95 – Klaus Koch: 9 u, 22 u, 47, 63 u – Rainer Kunert:
67 (3x) – LMU München: 71 u – Münchner Olympiapark GmbH:
79 o (3x) – Münchner Stadtmuseum: 52 – Museum Mensch und
Natur: 55 u – Volker Pfeifle: Umschlag hinten – Prähistorische
Staatssammlung: 56 (3x) – Ulrike Romeis: 32 lo, 33 u, 35 l –
Städtische Galerie im Lenbachhaus: 53 – Rudolf Sterflinger: 1 –
Verlagsarchiv: 25 ro, 27 lo (2x), 30 u (2x), 33 lo, 34 (2x), 39 lo,
41 o, 42 l, 57 o, 60 o, 71 o (2x), 73 u (2x), 75 (6x), 85 o
Erklärung: o: oben, u: unten, m: Mitte, l: links, r: rechts

ISBN-Nummer 3-930572-01-X